CAT
TWEETS

An Hachette UK Company
www.hachette.co.uk

First published in Great Britain in 2016
by Spruce, a division of
Octopus Publishing Group Ltd
Carmelite House, 50 Victoria
Embankment, London, EC4Y 0DZ
www.octopusbooks.co.uk
www.octopusbooksusa.com

Distributed in the US by
Hachette Book Group,
1290 Avenue of the Americas,
4th and 5th Floors, New York, NY 10020

Distributed in Canada by
Canadian Manda Group, 664 Annette St.
Toronto, Ontario, Canada M6S 2C8

Copyright © Octopus Publishing Group
Ltd 2016

ISBN 978-1-84601-535-9

A CIP catalogue record for this book
is available from the British Library.

Printed and bound in China
10 9 8 7 6 5 4 3 2 1

Publisher: Sarah Ford
Design: Jaz Bahra, Eoghan O'Brien
Editorial Assistant: Francesca Leung
Production Controller: Sarah Kulasek-
  Boyd
Picture Research: Giulia Hetherington,
  Jennifer Veall

Picture acknowledgements:

Emoji Graphics Copyright (2014) Twitter, Inc and other
contributors. The emojis used in this book are Twitter Emoji
(Twemoji) graphics, which are licensed under CC-BY 4.0: https://
creativecommons.org/licenses/by/4.0/Alamy Bailey-Cooper
Photography 16 above; Dmitriy Shironosov 18 above; Dunrobin
Studios/Stockimo 24 below; Helene Rogers/Art Directors & TRIP
30 above; Manfred Grebler 58 above; Martin Garnham 29 below;
Roger Bamber 15 above; Russell Hunter 29 above. Dreamstime.
com Alena Ozerova 55 above; Allnaturalbeth 61 below; Annamiro
1 (used throughout); Anna Yakimova 9 below; Artshock 33
below; Bakusova 50 below; Ben Schonewille 48 above, 62
above; Cheryl Davis 46 above; Chrisgandy 49 below; Constantin
Opris 11 below, 53 above; Dadachanz 35 below, 40 below; Dario
Rota 1 (used throughout); Darkbird77 31 below; David Milligan
12 below; Davidtb 31 above, 37 below, 38 below, 48 below, 62
below; Divajo 36 below; Duskbabe 52 below; Dzmitry Marhun
44 above; Ekaterina Cherkashina 51 below; Elenazarubina
45 below; Erik Lam 8 below, 13 below; Ermolaevamariya 55
below; Fotograf77 59 above; Fottoo 50 below; Hannadarzy 21
below; Helior 17 below; Igor Korionov 63 below; Isselee 7 below;
Jmcclung81 57 below; Joanna Zaleska 59 below; Jorge Pereira
60 below; Kanokrut Tesakarn 14 below; Kok Tiann Shyong 7
above; Leonidikan 24 above; Lunary 6 below; Maciej Czekajewski
44 below; Makapaktaeva 26 above; Malivoja 26 below; Marco
Guidi 10 below; Michael Galli 20 below; Michelangelo Oprandi
34 below; MNStudio 42 above; Nobilior 53 below; Olyapo 23
below; Pannawat Muangmoon 46 below; Pimmimemom 30
below; Pixbull 41 below; Pramot Pantadet 43 below; Said Tayar
Segundo 54 below; Santipap Watcharayothin 58 below; Sergey
Taran 49 above; Sjankauskas 63 above; Svetoslav Sokolov 25
below; Syda Productions 39 below; Tdhster 18 below; Tero
Hakala 19 below; Thomas Brandt 16 below; Tzooka 21 above;
Valeriya Potapova 56 below; Valery Vasiliev 42 below; Vallorie
Francis 32 below; Veronika Mannova 25 above; Videodeka 64
below; Vincenzo Marco Vallilonga 15 above; Vvita 43 above;
Zanna Peshnina 47 above, 47 below. Getty Images 101cats 8
above; Andriy Onufriyenko 34 above; anniepaddington 54 above;
Benjamin Torode 51 above; Benne Ochs 6 above; GK Hart/
Vikki Hart 14 above, 38 above; Image Source 60 above; John
Lund 12 above, 35 above, 36 above, 37 above; junku 17 above,
40 above; Kelly Bowden 11 above; Mike Brown 64 above; Photo
by marianna armata 20 above; retales botijero 10 above; Sean
Kernan 19 above; Sean Marc Lee 39 above; Shioguchi 9 above;
Tancrediphoto.com 33 above; Thomas Hong/EyeEm 32 above;
Tim Platt 13 above. istockphoto.com andersboman 61 above;
fbosse 45 above; y_bashar_babur 57 above. REX Shutterstock
KeystoneUSA-ZUMA 56 above; Peter Smith 41 above; Simon
Webster 52 above. Shutterstock Oleg Sytin 22 above; pio3 22
below; Rita Kochmarjova 23 above. Thinkstock lexxizm 27
above; Lulamej 28 below; Martin Poole 28 below; Ramonespelt
27 below; Rasulovs 1, 3. © Trevor Davies 2016 5 above, 5 below.

CAT
TWEETS

LOOK OUT, THE CATS HAVE
TAKEN TO TWITTER!

TREVOR DAVIES
AND HIS FELINE FRIENDS

**There are many things the feline of the species can do...
bio-mechanical engineering, playing Chopin's Études on
the piano, solving some of the trickiest sudokus ever
created, zumba... they just choose not to.**

In fact, such is the contrary nature of cats, that — as they peer down
at you from the shed roof and you undermine your public dignity by
cooing baby noises in their direction — they refuse to answer you.
Partly because to speak would break the "Cat Code" and gift insight
to their master plan for total species domination, and partly because
you're an idiot. Instead, your cat looks at you and runs through your
life, contentedly reliving all the mistakes you made in your career, love
life, financial planning, and social interactions — like a kind of fur-lined
feudal king smug in the knowledge that, had you really been in control
of things, you'd be on the shed roof too looking down on the idiots.

So it is scarcely a surprise that cats can tweet... should they wish to.
Here I have gathered the best of their supposed telecommunications
in order to give you an idea of how they function and their role within
the social petwork. I've done this in consultation with Frazzle... my very
own Guardian of my Inadequacies. On the face of it, Frazzle has little to
do and thus communicate about, but when I put this to her, her stare
was enough to make me understand that the burden of her duties was
frankly beyond my understanding.

There was the ironing to re-fur, the litter to re-distribute around
the kitchen floor, the postman wouldn't frown at himself, wedding
photos needed upending (not in a fit of jealousy, but more a callous
protestation at the honeymoon she spent in the cattery), there were

slippers to attack, the stair carpet needs scratching at 3am each morning, and the freshly laid herb garden needed "fertilizing". Such is the onerous weight of duty laid at her door, there's little wonder that cats' default response to our communications is incredulity.

In this book you'll see exactly how the most antisocial of species communicates its feelings about you, your stupid world, your stupid other pets, and the stupid habits that you think civilization has spent thousands of years perfecting, but are in fact an eternity of compounded errors. From these tweets, I hope you will understand that the world that you so glibly tweet about isn't full of glossy-eyed, adoring fans, obediently "favoriting" and "retweeting", but a master species biding their time, feeding on your inadequacies, mocking the smallest failures (have you ever seen your cat watching you exercise?), relishing your self-destructive pretensions, watching as you stare at your phones in hope that someone cares, and building towards the day of reckoning... but only if they can be bothered.

Frazzle
@OwnedByAnIdiot

Just checked on the world from the shed roof... it's pitiful, but mine.

FROM CHEZ DAVIES

5

Zeppelin
@FrequentDeliquent

Happy Chinese New Year!
#yearofthemouse

Davina
@AngryOverture

Finally got to grips with parenting.
#shouldhavebeenspayed

 Bear Frills
@AllTerrainPaws

You know those times when you regret climbing to the top of the lavatory door?! #cant_unsee_this

Chippendale
@50ADayHabit

I love a martini with an extravagant garnish.

 Twilight Tequila
@Twittertroll

@Beezer was thrilled with the new bonnet I knitted him. @Prudence has integrity issues.

Viscount Buzz Paws
@MonocleOfMau

OK guys, I've checked and nowhere is it written that we aren't the superior species... so let's just assume.

FROM HIGHER ACADEMY OF STUFF THAT WE KNOW LIBRARY

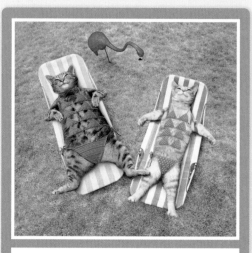

 Pinot Gnaw
@SixFigureAlimony

Enid wanted to go topless, but it's not that kind of neighborhood.

Coal Bucket
@SunnySideUp

That little furry thing was in the kitchen again! Someone oughta do something. #trésunhygienic.

 Buster Futon
@TheyDrewFirstBlood

This used to be a lot more fun before the computer age.

Gemima
@CarbsBeforeBedtime

I 💚 cookery shows.

Arnie
@LikeTotallyAwesome

Mistakenly achieved the 80s rock look through not blow-drying.

 Buffy
@AngriestLampshade

When I grow into a tiger, they die.

 Walter
@HalfGlassOfDreams

Feel I really stood out at the stage auditions for *Watership Down*. Fingers crossed.

 Missy Tinsel Bomb
@MouseSeeTongue

Now I know why you shouldn't play with your food... it's really boring!

Percy
@PlatinumButterKnife

**Don't ya just hate it when you drop
your spoon in your bouillabaisse?**

Colditz
@FatesPunchBag

When @Fleapit's collar comes off I'm gonna need to find a new itching post... and possibly a new home.

 Attilla the Paw
@FullFatFinch

In bad need of Imodium® after happening across an unguarded cocktail sausage. #workingitthrough

FROM SOMEWHERE NEAR THE LITTER TRAY

Cuthbert
@SpiderCat

She's defrosted prawns!

Badger Talbot
@BadgerCull

Big night on the tiles with @FlufflesMcGrew. #sickasapig

FROM FLUFFLES' CRIB

 Barfly
@Oddjob

My wing man @Bismark and me are
exhausted after licking the dishes
clean! #moneysavingchores

Piccalilli
@PicklesThePious

For what I'm about to steal from the kitchen worktop, may the Lord make me eternally fat and dozy.

Bernadette
@ConfluenceOfNeuroses

Note to self: Never take a selfie at the top of the basement stairs.

SnowQueenFairyDust
@NamedByAToddler

Just tried vegetarian kibble.

 Dweezle
@CosmoTheDestroyer

I simply can't help myself...
#wired-at-auntie-mauds-funeral

FROM PAWS-FOR-THOUGHT PET CREMATORIUM

Tucker
@Only2LivesLeft

Can't believe they were keeping this place from me all this time. #cozy

FROM THE BIG CLAY BED IN THE BACK YARD

 Tricktionary
@BigAirPaws

I like totally just landed a sick backside 360.

FROM CAT FLIP SKATE PARK

 Maynard
@ClickerTubs

I spent a fortune on this equipment
and the image is tiny!

FROM PICTURE PAWS FILM SCHOOL

Jennifer Juniper
@TheLittlestBoho

Remembered to tick "non-smoker"
on my online dating profile, but
forgot to tick "no dogs".

FROM DOWN AT THE END OF LONELY STREET

 Anastasia Sequined Footspa
@HarshButFair

Hopefully this will keep people's attention from her hideous haircut.

FROM ATOP AN IDIOT

Pippa Pearlypaws
@EthicalVacuum

Not sure it was the tattoo's position or what it depicted that so shocked the girls.

FROM BIBLE STUDY GROUP

Suzy Sue
@Sue'n'Army

Why does he keep going on about
the kids' hamster? It wasn't even that
tasty.

Pericles
@PerryMySon

Not sure my book club enjoyed my choice of *Twinkle Goes to the Vet.*

FROM EAST COMPTON EVENING CLASS

 Emperor Door Knob
@AttitudeMalfunction

My first attempt at canine surgery on a sleeping hound!! Here goes nothing. #clawslikescalpels

 Blinky
@AdventuresInFurnishings

It's cozy, but it doesn't smell like my bed.

$_z{}^zZ$

FROM CALVIN KLEIN'S HAMMOCK

 Oven Glove
@DreamOfTheDivine
BuddhaCat

Another brave attempt from Colin to reach the canapés.

FROM THE DINNER PARTY KITCHEN

Busby
@AngryTillTuesday

If we had got cable, I wouldn't have to do this.

🙀 🙀 🙀

FROM FOUR FLOORS NEARER THE SUN

Ernest Eric
@VersatileVeracity

She doesn't look happy. Said I'd be
back by 10. #sleepingwiththedog

Piffle
@FurLinedProdigy

Just learned what spayed means!

FROM THE LIBRARY (EAST WING)

 Bandit
@DamCandy

So disappointing when the boys don't put any effort into a game of hide-and-seek.

David Meeowy
@MinorTom

Nope, that's just too much effort... I'll carry on using my tongue.

FROM EN SUITE LITTER TRAY

Kerouac
@DesolateAngel

It may look like I've just graduated,
but they are just using me to serve
drinks at the barbecue.

 Ewok
@LookAtThisThing
ThatIBring

Ew, I'd forgotten what I trod in!
#duganoldhole

Squid
@FelineProvidence

**If you're up there send me a sign!
A fat, feathery, unsuspecting sign!**

FROM THE VICARAGE GARDEN

 Madam La La
@LetsDiscussMyDisgust

Heated seat, designer tiles, autoflush...
and they expect me to use that?

FROM THE SMALLEST ROOM

Troy
@OddyPuss

I have returned from my travels to find the family is as stupid as they were when I set out.

Lee Burt Archie
@TwinklePaws

Perhaps "Sympathy for the Devil" was the wrong choice for the church piano recital.

FROM FEAR AND COOKIES HOLY DISCIPLES OF CHRIST FREE CHURCH

 Crackers
@WhoDaresPanics

**Slipped into something more
Christmassy! #pleasehelp**

Astro
@BacksideRadiation

First pole dancing lesson! Lots of sniffing and spraying, but no dancing yet.

FROM MADAME SHAKETAIL'S ACADEMY OF THE EXOTIC

Shylock
@DefaultIncredulity

Surely he must have more than one pair! Why does he have to take them off and wash them now?

FROM LAUNDRY CIRCLE OF HELL

Meatloaf
@SnoozeControl

It said "Tiger-sized cat bed" on Amazon, but Orson can barely squeeze his fat butt in.

 Dunstan
@BiscuitBasedLifeForm

Regretting demonstrating
chin-up reps on a first date. Didn't
get beyond three and she's having
to phone the fire brigade.

FROM DOGDUMP PARK

 Augustus McFlurry
@OneCatSympawsium

Just explained the birds and the bees to young @Butterscotch. Chase both, but only eat the former.

 Comet
@ModestMegastar

Once up here, it wasn't nearly as easy to steer as Nigel made out.

 Dylan
@CollegeDropout

Just had another festive sausage dream. #puttingupthedreamdecs

Kayleigh
@HumilityBypass

Moments after taking this photo my new latrine turned into the scariest shower I've ever had.

FROM SHINIEST CUPBOARD IN THE KITCHEN

Prunella
@CatSizedTyrant

If I've doctored that dog lead properly, only one of them should return from the walk.

FROM PRUNELLA'S LAIR

Post

Oswald
@OzTheOverAchiever

**The boys have arrived in Acapulco!
Let the good times begin.**

FROM PLAYA DEL CARNAL SORTING OFFICE

Courtney
@CatnessEverDream

Rather than discuss the Shopping
Channel purchases, I decided to play
dead. #sharedcreditcard

FROM THE CRIME SCENE

Jackpot
@HairballInHell

If @Tizer's correct, in 5 minutes' time we will be gorging ourselves on leftover sushi... if he isn't, we'll be covered in used litter.

FROM LOCATION IS CLASSIFIED